Sewing: Sewing fc

Your Ultimate Step by Step Easy to Follow Guide with Clear Instructions and Illustrations

Introduction

I want to thank you and congratulate you for downloading the book, *"Sewing: Sewing for Beginners, Your Ultimate Step by Step Easy to Follow Guide with Clear Instructions and Illustrations"*.

This book contains proven steps and strategies on how to sew.

Anyone can learn how to sew. This book is full of instructions and illustrations specifically targeted for beginners to teach them how to sew. The step by step guides are so easy to follow, even children can do it. Grab you needle and thread and get ready to learn how to sew!

Thanks again for downloading this book, I hope you enjoy it!

Chapter 1

Basic Information and Tools Needed for Sewing

Sewing is a fun activity that fuels creativity and challenges the mind. There are so many uses for sewing. You can make a dress or a bag for your personal use. You can make curtains and pillow covers for the home. Anything that can be joined together using a needle and thread can be sewn. The possibilities are endless once you know how to sew.

The basic principle of sewing is joining two fabrics together using a stitch to make something out of these sewn together fabrics. It sounds simple so there's no reason why you cannot learn to sew.

Simple Sewing Kit

There are so many sewing tools available on the market today. For this portion, the focus is on identifying the basic tools that should be in your sewing kit. You can add more and build on these items as you progress your sewing lesson.

1. Tape Measure – Use the tape measure to take body measurements, fabric measurements, and seam measurements. A measuring tape made of plastic will work quite well because it is inexpensive and will not stretch.
2. Needles – These refer to needles used to sew by hand. Needles are usually sold in a set and each set contains different sizes to help you tackle any project that needs hand sewing. The available sizes are 1-12. Generally, hand sewing uses sizes 6 to 9.
3. Pins – Pins are used to hold the fabric together before sewing it. They come in plain or colorful tips to make it easier for you to see them when they are pinned onto a fabric.
4. Threads – Threads come in different colors and are usually made of polyester-cotton blends. There are also metallic, wool, and embroidery threads for different kinds of sewing projects.
5. Seam Ripper – If you made a mistake sewing a stitch, a seam ripper or a stitch ripper can remove the stich for you. Keep the cover on at all times because the sharp point can hurt you.
6. Scissors – If possible, buy 2 types of scissors: one only for cutting fabric and one for trimming and cutting threads.
7. Thimble – A thimble protects your finger when hand sewing.
8. Needle Threader – This thin wire is shaped like an arrowhead and can help you insert the thread into the needle.

9. Tailor's Chalk – marks the fabric and can be easily washed off.
10. Container – find a container for your sewing kit that's lightweight, easy to carry, and can fit all the items listed above. A see-through container will help you asses what's in your sewing kit immediately.

Some additional items you will need but won't fit in your kit includes an iron and ironing board, some buttons and other fasteners, patterns, and fabric.

The Sewing Machine

A sewing machine can help complete any sewing project faster than sewing by hand. Sewing machines nowadays are computerized and have a library of stitches ready to use at a press of a button. The list below contains sewing machine parts that most electronic sewing machines usually have. Consult your machine's manual should you not find the part in the list below. There may be extra features on your sewing machine that can be handy when you are sewing.

1. Thread Guide – guides that mark where your threads should go
2. Tension Dial – controls how fast the upper thread feeds into the sewing machine
3. Spool Holder – holds the thread
4. Bobbin Winder – winds the thread from the spool into a bobbin.
5. Balance Wheel or Hand Wheel – Manually moves the needle up or down
6. Stitch Selection Guide – Different types of stitches that your sewing machine is capable of making. Electronic sewing machines usually have a screen display and more types of stitches than old models
7. Reverse Stitch Indicator – is a lever or a button that reverses your stitch
8. Needle – Uses thread to make a stitch
9. Presser Foot – Presses the fabric flat on the needle plate
10. Needle Plate - A needle plate is made of metal and sits under the presser foot and the needle
11. Dog Feeds – Moves the fabric forward
12. Bobbin Cover – is a clear plastic cover that can be opened and closed to access the bobbin.
13. Bobbin – holds the lower thread that feeds into the machine as you stitch.

These are the parts for a basic sewing machine. Other machines like an edging machine called a serger and embroidery machines have parts that a regular sewing machine do not have. Sergers and embroidery machines are usually used by professional tailors and sewers.

Chapter 2

A Lesson in Fabrics

Fabrics are essential to making clothes, craft projects and covering home furnishings. They are made of fibers that are woven together to form a continuous piece of cloth that can be cut and shaped to form patterns that you stitch together to make clothes.

Choosing the right fabric for your sewing project means taking into consideration how suitable the fabric is for the project. For example, a fabric made of thick material like tweed is more suitable for making sofa covers than using a thin fabric like organza which can break easily and is too slippery.

Consider also the cost and care for the clothes you are going to make. If you want to make a dress for a child, opt for cotton fabrics instead of synthetic. These are breathable and can be easily washed as children tend to make a mess on their clothes. Cotton fabrics are inexpensive and great for everyday wear.

Listed below are the most common fabrics used in making clothes and soft furnishings. Find out which fabric best suits you.

Cotton Fabrics – Cotton fabrics are the most common and most widely used fabrics of them all. They can be used in almost any type of clothing or sewing project. Cotton fabrics are used mainly for making clothes. They absorb moisture very well and can keep you cool in the summer. Cotton fabrics are easy to dye that's why you can have more color choices when choosing from cotton fabrics. On the downside, cotton fabrics are prone to shrinking, gets wrinkled and soiled easily. Some of the most common cotton fabrics are chambray, corduroy, denim, gingham, jersey, muslin and terry cloth. These can be used to make dresses, shirts and pants and can be easily washed using any regular washing machine.

Silk Fabrics – silk fabrics make up some of the most luxurious fabrics ever made. They come from fibers off a silkworm's cocoon. Silk fabrics require careful handling as they can be sometimes very delicate and tear easily. They also dye very well. Silk fabrics are used for making wedding gowns or clothes used for special occasions. Sometimes they are used for making blouses and dresses too. Chiffon, georgette, organza, satin and taffeta are some of the most common silk fabrics used for these types of clothes. Most silk fabrics are dry clean only.

Synthetic Fabrics – Synthetic fabrics are fabrics that are made by man. This means that they are not derived from any natural sources like plant fiber or animal wool. Most synthetic fibers are inexpensive and do not absorb well. Because synthetic fabrics are not made with natural fibers, they don't breathe well and can make you feel hot when you are wearing them under the sun. They are often mixed with cotton and other natural fibers to make the clothes less expensive. Some synthetic fabrics mimic the feel of a natural fabric but do not perform as well. Most synthetic fabrics have a little bit of stretch in them so they require threads or stitching that can accommodate the stretch. Nylon, Polyester, rayon and spandex are some synthetic fabrics you might know.

Wool Fabrics – Wool fabrics are most often made from woolen fleece sheared off a sheep. It can also come from wool fibers off a goat's fur, rabbit's fur, llamas and camel hair. Wool fabrics are breathable. It keeps you warm in a cold winter and cool during a hot summer. Wool fabrics are flame resistant and are very absorbent. To make wool less expensive, they are mixed with other fibers. Wool fabrics are used to make coats, jackets, capes, sweaters and soft furnishings. Cashmere, crepe, flannel and tweed are some of the most common wool fabrics used.

Choose the right fabric for your sewing project. Go to a fabric store and touch and feel the fabric before buying it. Do not buy fabric in bulk unless you are undertaking a sewing project that requires a lot of fabric. When buying thread, bring a sample of the fabric or a swatch to compare the thread with.

Chapter 3

Basic Hand and Machine Stitches

Now that you have the sewing kit, know the parts of your sewing machine, and have some idea about what fabric to choose, it's time to try them all out. This chapter is about learning how to make basic hand and machine stitches.

The first thing you need to do is to thread the needle. You can either make a single thread or a double thread.

To make a single thread, take one end of the thread and slide it into the eye of the needle. Pull the thread 3-4 inches through the needle and tie a knot at the longer end. Always be on the lookout for the shorter end while you are sewing lest it will slip through and you'll need to rethread it again. The length of the thread should not exceed 18 inches to avoid getting the thread in knots.

Another way to thread a needle is to do a double thread. Pull one end through the eye of the needle until the length on both ends are equal. Make a knot using both threads.

To secure a thread at the end of your stitch so that it will not unravel, do a simple stitch and go back through the stitch. Move your needle through the hole that it creates before pulling it all in. This will create a knot at the fabric.

Hand Stitches

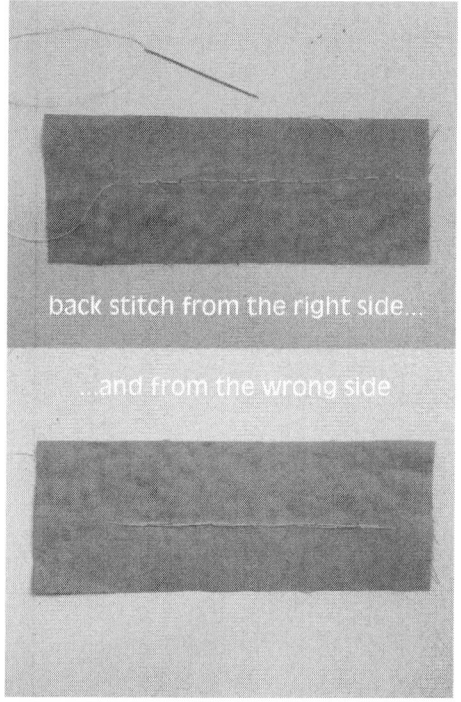
back stitch from the right side...
...and from the wrong side

Hand stitches are very useful for when you need to mend a tear or decorate a fabric and when you don't have a sewing machine available. For this lesson, the hand stitches detailed below are the most basic stitches you will need to connect two fabrics together.

The most basic hand stitch is called a running stitch. To make a running stitch, push a threaded needle from wrong side or the back side of the fabric to the front of the fabric. Pull on the thread until you reach the knot. Plunge it back to the fabric a few millimeters away to make a straight line. Allot some space similar to the size of your first stitch and repeat the process going from right to left of the fabric. Your end result should look like a broken line.

Make the lines longer than a few millimeters, around ¼ to ½ inch, to make a basting stitch. A basting stitch is used to hold the fabric in place prior to running it through a sewing machine. This is similar to putting pins on the fabrics except in this case, you use a single thread to hold the fabrics together loosely. That thread will later on be removed once you have stitched the fabric through the sewing machine.

The next stitch is called a back stitch. Start by making a running stitch and doubling back by filling in the gaps with another running stitch. It is called a back stitch because you are going back through the stitch to make a straight line. This is the closest stitch you can compare to a machine stitch and is usually sturdier than a running stitch.

Blanket stitches are used to make the edge of the fabric look neat. To make a blanket stitch, go to the left edge of the fabric and pull the thread at the top left corner of the fabric. From the same side, just a few millimeters to the right, pull the thread until it makes a short line at the edge of the fabric. Hold the thread with your left index finger and plunge the needle a few millimeters below to make a 90 degree angle. Thread the needle back to where your index finder is holding the thread to make a loop. Repeat until you reach the end.

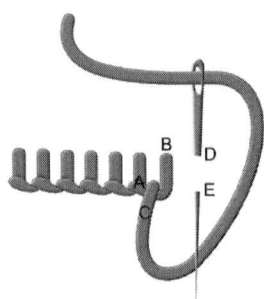

A herringbone stitch is used to secure hems on skirts and slacks. Start by folding the hem of the skirt by ½ inch and pressing on it so that it stays flat. From under the folded side, thread a needle. Make a diagonal line and thread the needle to the non-folded side such that the needle is poking out from visible part of the skirt. Pull it back in a few millimeters to the left and then plunge it on the folded part diagonally. Repeat until you have gone through the entire hem. Your end product should look like a zigzag over the edge of the folded hem inside the skirt.

HERRINGBONE

Machine Stitches

Machine stitches are easier to do than hand stitches. It usually doesn't require you to learn how to make the stitch. You just have to select the right machine stitch from the stitch selection based on what you need.

The straight stitch is the most basic and most widely used among all the machine stitches. It is similar to a backstitch but more polished and even looking. Use this stitch to make seams and connect fabrics together.

Select the zigzag stitch from your sewing machine's stitch selection guide when you need to neaten the edge or make decorative stitches on your fabric. A zigzag stitch can also be used for appliqués (meaning sewing a piece of fabric on top of another fabric).

A blind hem stitch is used similar to a herringbone stitch such that the stitch cannot be seen from the front.

A buttonhole stitch as the name implies is used to make buttonholes. Cut the in the middle to make a hole. In electronic sewing machines, the size of the buttonhole can be adjusted.

There are 3 common types of buttonhole stitch. The basic buttonhole looks like a rectangle with a line in the middle. It is the most common among the three. The round-end buttonhole has one end rounded. The last is the keyhole buttonhole stitch which has one square end and one shaped like a loop thus the name keyhole. Both round-end and keyhole are used for jackets.

Decorative stitches vary with every sewing machine. They can be a shape of a flower or a more complex zigzag. Choose these stitches when you want to decorate the edge of your sleeves, bottom of your shirts and pants. Use different colored thread to make it more interesting.

There are more kinds of stitches out there that you can learn. Do not limit yourself to only a few stitches. Different stitches have different uses in sewing.

Chapter 4

Fasteners

Buttons and zippers are the most common fasteners that you can use. They can be functional and decorative at the same time. These and other fasteners are detailed below.

1. Buttons – Buttons are used on all kinds of clothing. Buttons can be plastic, metal, shanked and even the same fabric as the clothing. These are called covered buttons.
2. Zippers – Zippers, like buttons, can be used to fasten all kinds of clothing. The types of zippers are regular, invisible, open ended and decorative.
    a. Regular zippers or centered zippers are used for blouses, skirts and slacks.
    b. Invisible zippers are used for dresses, gowns and whenever you don't want your zipper to be visible.
    c. Open ended zippers are used for jackets that need to be opened completely.
    d. Decorative zippers are used for bags and tops to make them more interesting.
3. Hook and Eye - These are used to fasten a skirt or slacks.
4. Hook and Looped Eye – These are slightly smaller versions of the hook and eye and are used for bras, dresses and skirts with no bands.
5. Snap Fastener – Snap fasteners are 2 tiny metal fasteners that snap together to close a blouse or a pocket. These can be used in place of a button if you don't want the fasteners to be seen.
6. Velcro – Velcros are used for overalls and board shorts. They come in different colors and sizes to suit your needs. They are usually made of cloth so they can be easily sewn on to fabrics.
7. Snap Tape – You might find these on jogging pants of athletes. These are small round snaps that are sewn into a single strip of cloth and sewn on the sides of their jogging pants. Notice how athletes just remove their track pants quickly. Snap tapes make it possible.
8. Eyelet – Eyelets are not technically fasteners. But when you loop a ribbon through it, it becomes a part of a corset. These are mostly used for gowns and lingerie.

How to Sew on a Button

To sew on a button with 2 holes, simply line up the button on the fabric. Marking underneath the button with a tailor's chalk can help make sure they are aligned. Using a double thread, start under the button and through the first hole. Place a toothpick on top of the button and loop the thread over it before threading it to the other hole. Repeat the process 5-7 times ending at underneath the button. Wrap the thread under the button to make a shank and then stitch back to the fabric to close.

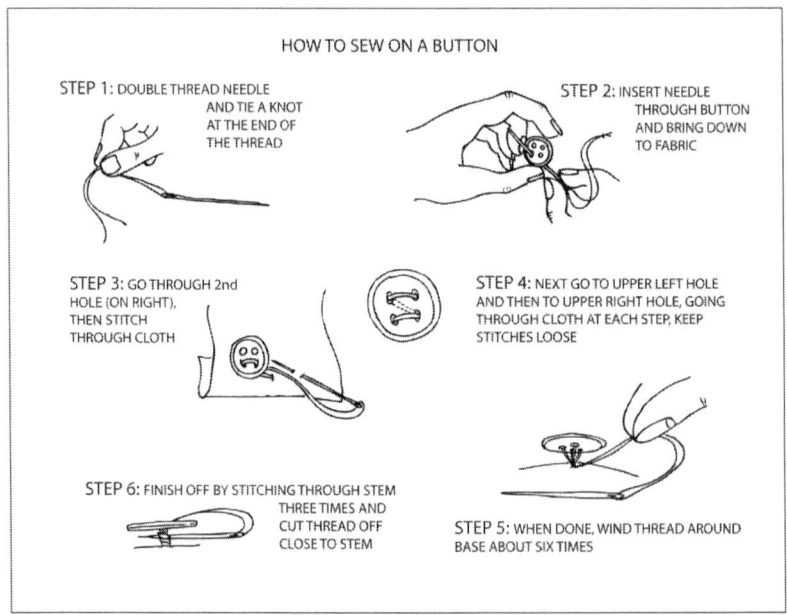

The same process applies to 4 holed buttons. The difference lies on whether you want the threads to look like an x mark or 2 small parallel lines on top of the button.

To sew on a shanked button, align the buttons using a tailor's chalk. Use a double thread to loop around the shank of the button. Repeat 5-7 times and stitch back into the fabric to close.

How to Sew a Zipper

Start by stitching together the seams of 2 fabrics leaving a gap at the top for the zipper. Open the seam allowance (around ½ an inch) and press them to flatten them. Place center of the zipper on the gap. Make sure the zipper is closed. You may baste the gap so that it doesn't move too much as you sew on the zipper. Stitch the zipper onto the seam allowance using your sewing machine. On the visible side of the fabric where the zipper opens, stich around the zipper starting from the top left going down the length of the zipper and then back up again. The zipper should look like it is encased in a narrow rectangle.

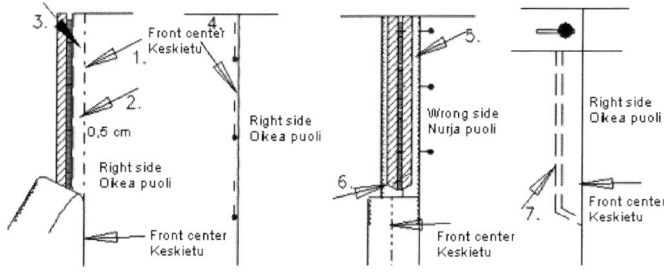

Chapter 5

Mending Your Clothes

Besides making clothes, sewing is essentially used for mending clothes. When your shirt is torn, slashed or ripped, there's no need to throw them away just yet. Using some simple sewing techniques, your ripped clothing can still be used just like before.

Mending a Tear

A vertical or horizontal tear can happen if a sharp object slashes through your clothing. To mend this tear, cut a piece of fusing to the length of the tear. Fusing can be bought at all fabric stores. Use a zigzag stitch over the torn side going thru the fusing. Make sure you use the same color thread as your fabric to make it less noticeable.

Making a Patch

A patch is a great way to mend a big tear or a hole on the fabric. To make a patch, find the closest color fabric to the original fabric on the cloth. Cut the patch in a square big enough to cover the whole tear or hole. Baste or pin the patch onto the fabric to prevent the patch from moving. Using a zigzag stitch, stich all four sides of the patch on top of the tear or hole. Use the same color thread to make the patch less noticeable or use contrasting thread to make it look like a decorative patch.

For patterned fabrics or fabrics with designs, cut a square around the tear or hole. Fold the raw edges under by a few millimeters and press on it so that it doesn't move. Cut a patch in the same design or grain as the square. Place the patch underneath the square hole and baste. Using small stitches, stitch together the folded raw edges with the patch using the closest color thread. The patch should look like it blends in with the design of the fabric.

Mending a Tear with a Fusible Appliqué

Sometimes, a tear in your clothing can become an opportunity to add designs to it. This is mostly done on children's clothing. To repair a tear using a fusible appliqué, simply pin the design on top of the tear and apply heat. The fusible appliqué should adhere to the fabric once heat is applied.

Mending a Broken Zipper

When you put too much strain on a zipper, they can break and might need to be replaced with a new zipper. If only a few "teeth" of the zipper is broken, this can still be mended using a thread and a needle. Start by closing the zipper up to the top. You have to feed the teeth carefully on the zipper so that it doesn't unravel. Once it is closed, hand stitch just a few teeth above the broken teeth. This way, the zipper puller will stop at the stitch.

Mending a Split Seam

A split seam is common to pants and blouses. To mend a split seam, use a seam ripper to remove the stitching on either side of the split seam. Cut a piece of fusing tape and place over the split seam. Re-stitch the seam over the fusing tape with the same color as the fabric.

Mend a Hole on Knitted Clothing

To mend a hole on knitted clothing, use a wool yarn in the same color of the cloth. If the knitted clothing allows ironing, iron at the wrong side of the garment to make the hole flat. Make running stitches around the hole so that it forms an oval shape surrounding the hole. Then make horizontal running stitches inside the oval shape until the hole no longer opens.

Mending clothes can save you money in the long run. It can give new life to torn clothes making them useful again. Your favorite dress doesn't need to be thrown away once it has been mended. In this age of materialism, mending is sometimes not considered. Mend your clothes instead of throwing them away. It will save you money and it will save the environment by lessening the trash you make.

Chapter 6

More Tips and Tricks

There are hundreds of tips and tricks for any type of sewing project. Here are some more tips and tricks to make sewing easier and faster.

1. When threading a needle, use wax to straighten the thread and make it easy to slip into the eye of the needle. Use a needle threader if available.
2. If you need a guide for difficult hand stitches or just to make them look even, use a machine baste stitch on the fabric and remove later on when you have finished sewing on the hand stitch.
3. Browse through men's wear discount shops for shirts that are on sale and repurpose them to make blouses. Men's shirts are big enough to make new blouses and are cheaper than department store bought women's blouses.
4. Before cutting a fabric, lay down all the pattern pieces and pin it on the fabric. Be sure to save space and use the little spaces in between bigger pattern pieces for pockets, patches, collars and cuffs.
5. For tough fabrics like leather, use the side of a ruler or a stitching grove to mark the line which you will stich on. This ensures that the line will be straight. Follow up with a stitching wheel to mark the spaces between each stich to make it even. Use an awl to pierce the leather before stitching.
6. Use zigzag stitches for hemming knits. Zigzag stitches allow for stretching of the fabric.
7. Pillowcases sold in thrift stores for less than a dollar can be used for any kind of sewing project. Buy the white ones and make simple shirts for children. Buy patterned and even embroidered pillowcases and make skirts and shirts with designs.
8. Same as the pillow cases, thrift stores also sell sheets at prices much lower than the department store prices. Choose sheets in plain colors to make a blouse or a shirt for an adult. You can make 2-3 items of clothing from one sheet alone.
9. If you lose a button on your blouse and cannot find a replacement button, change all of them to give your blouse a whole new look. Look for buttons that can contrast or compliment your blouse. Choose a button in a shiny finish to add a little elegance to your old blouse.
10. Buy the best threads that you can buy. Cheap threads easily break and even bleed into fabrics. High quality threads can be slightly expensive but will save you in the long run.
11. Pick patterns that can be used for different types of clothing. A round skirt pattern for example can double as a pattern for a Christmas tree skirt.
12. Instead of cutting on the pattern directly, trace patterns onto inexpensive craft paper and reuse them for bigger or smaller sizes.
13. Place patterns in similar craft envelopes to organize your patterns better.

14. Some fabrics have a tendency to shrink. Before sewing on a fabric, pre-treat or pre-wash them to ensure they do not shrink.
15. Test a fabric for bleeding. Red and black are especially prone to bleeding onto white or light colored fabrics.
16. Use the correct heat setting when pressing or ironing a fabric. Press or iron a swatch of the fabric before pressing on the finished product. You wouldn't want to burn your newly sewn dress, would you?
17. Clean your sewing machine by following the manufacturer's recommendation. Manual sewing machines need oiling once in a while.
18. Sew on ribbons on the edges and hems of jeans, skirts and blouses to make them look interesting. This is an inexpensive way to brighten up plain old clothing.
19. Cut the fabric on the right grain. This is for aesthetic and functional reasons.
20. Practice, practice, practice! All the expert seamstresses and tailors started out as a beginner at some point. Practice on scraps of cloth, use easy to manipulate fabrics for your initial projects and progress with tougher materials as you improve.

Conclusion

Sewing is a great hobby that you can do to make something out of nothing. It can be relaxing and rewarding activity all at the same time. If you find you are good at sewing, you can even make profit from making clothes for you and others. Just remember that it is not the end of the world if you make a mistake.

Don't be afraid of using your sewing machine or other imposing sewing tools. They are made to help you. Use the right tools and the right fabrics for all your sewing projects. Visit the internet and find online sites dedicated to sewing.

Learn from the pros and take classes if you have time. Don't be afraid to try a new sewing skill. The more you learn, the better your finished product looks like. Have fun sewing!

Thank you again for downloading this book!

Thank you and good luck!

Check out my other Best Selling Book From Margaret Smith

Preview of "The Ultimate Quilting Techniques for Beginners"

[Click Here to Check out the rest of "The Ultimate Quilting Techniques for Beginners"](#)

Or go to: http://amzn.to/1QNHXGM

Chapter 7: How to Make a Quilt

Now after having the required knowledge about quilting and the equipment, now in this section beginner will learn how to make their first quilt. You can make a quilt for any purpose, it can be a blanket or covering, but starting from a baby quilt would be appropriate because it requires less time and efforts. As you gain command over it you can move on to larger quilts. Following instruction and tips will help you in achieving the best out of your quilting efforts.

- Start by buying some few different fabrics. You can choose a multicolored floral fabric and then select other designs that can complement it.

- The rotary cutting tools are to be employed now. You can use the 6 inches by 24 inches ruler to cut down your fabric to 5.5 inches, which can be used for basic blocks for the quilt. At the crease fold your fabric in two halves, then put the ruler on the fabric. Now you can run the rotary cutting tool on your fabric along the ruler. This will make two blocks at a time of desired length and width. In this case it would be a square of 5.5 inches.

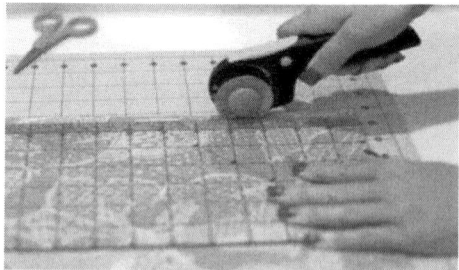

- You need 36 such squares for your baby quilt. Now it is time to assemble those pieces, you can assemble it on a floor or table that is spacious enough to hold all 36 pieces at a time. Swap and move the pieces around to make a pattern which pleases you.

- After you have decided the layout for the blocks of quilt, use the quilt pin to join the squares row by row together. Now use the sewing machine for stitching each of the squares with the next, with straight stitches and 0.25 inch inseam.

- After all the rows have been seamed together, use the iron to press the seam to flatten it. The seams should be ironed in one direction. Using seam lines as guide match the row with row below. Now make a straight stitch using the stitching machine and 0.25 inch inseam. After joining all 36 squares press the seams again.
- Now if you have followed the above instructions you should be ready to add the borders. The choice of borders is also up to you. Trim two strips of fabric that are 5 inches wide and 44 inches long. Join the strips on either side of the blocked quilt. Now trim off the length of the borders that is extra so that the border length matches with the length of stitched blocks. Use the machine to stitch 0.25 inch inseam with the blocks,

Congratulations! The quilt top for your quilt has been completed.

- Now the quilt sandwich is to be made. Put your backing fabric in some spacious place, keep in mind that the right side should be facing downwards. Put your batting on it, the batting can be of any type. There should be no wrinkles in the layers of quilt.

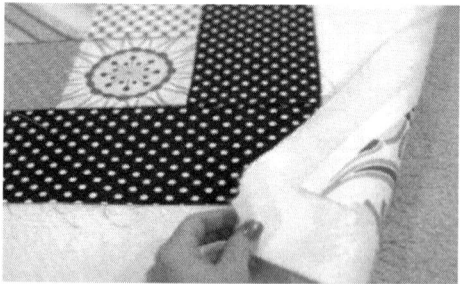

- It is time now to prepare your quilt for running through a quilting machine. For attaching all three layers of the quilt use large quilting safety pins. Use at least one pin per block to keep everything in place.

- Now sew your quilt blocks under the sewing machine with the aid of walking foot.

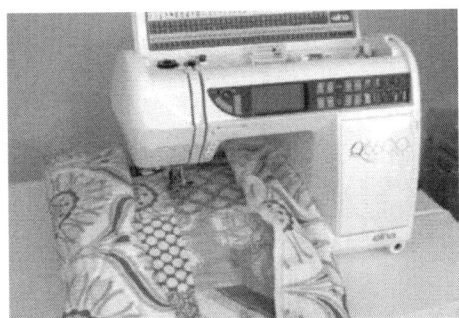

- Now square off the quilt by sewing around the perimeters. Just leave enough extra edge in order to fill the binding later on.

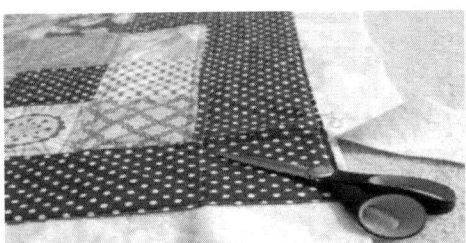

- Now is the time to create your binding. Select a piece of fabric from which you want to make your binding. Cut 44 inches long and 2.5 inches wide piece of that fabric. After cutting the fabric, machine stitch them at right angles to each other. There should be diagonal stitch from one side to other.

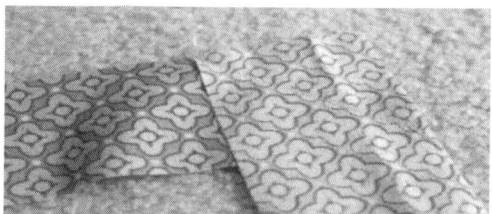

- Now use a scissor to trim off the little triangle off.

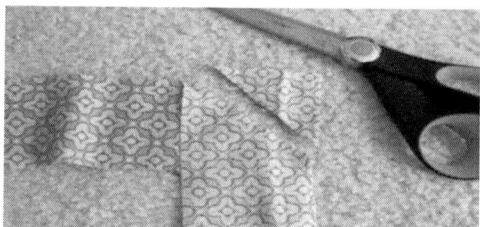

- Now unfold the sewn strips to form a continuous binding strip.

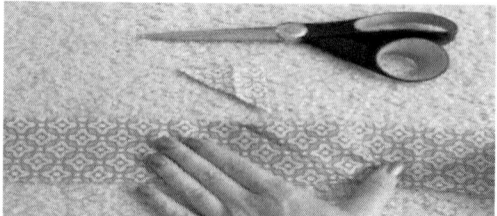

- Iron the binding strip to form a crease in half length wise.

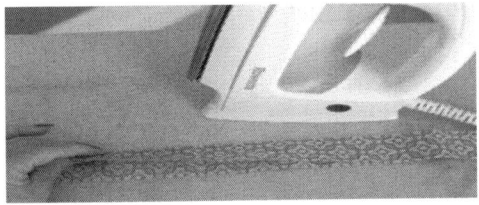

- Now use straight pins in order to pin the binding on the upper side of the quilt, keep the rough side outwards while the folded side should be facing inwards towards the middle of the quilt. Leave a 8 inch tail that should be hanging off the quilt and unpinned at the starting point.

- Make an upward folded triangle when you reach the corners.

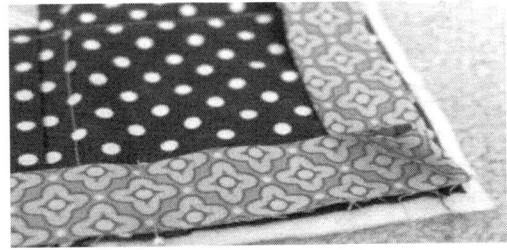

- Place pins in the triangles and two on their either sides. Once you have gone through entire quilt you need to join the strips. For this you need to fold the left strip down as shown.

- Now put the right strip in the folded strip piece.

Pin it to secure and machine stitch it around the edges. When you reach a corner, back stitch a little bit to secure. Lift the sewing foot and turn the quilt, again lower the foot and start to stitch again.

- Fold the binding to the backside of your quilt, use pin to secure and make use of the small needle and thread to stitch the binding to the back side of the quilt.

- After all the hard work, your quilt is now ready. This is what it might look like.

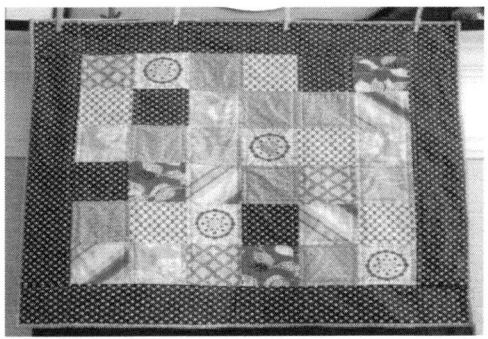

© Copyright 2014 by Angel Publishing Inc - All rights reserved.

This document is geared towards providing exact and reliable information in regards to the topic and issue covered. The publication is sold with the idea that the publisher is not required to render accounting, officially permitted, or otherwise, qualified services. If advice is necessary, legal or professional, a practiced individual in the profession should be ordered.

- From a Declaration of Principles which was accepted and approved equally by a Committee of the American Bar Association and a Committee of Publishers and Associations.

In no way is it legal to reproduce, duplicate, or transmit any part of this document in either electronic means or in printed format. Recording of this publication is strictly prohibited and any storage of this document is not allowed unless with written permission from the publisher. All rights reserved.

The information provided herein is stated to be truthful and consistent, in that any liability, in terms of inattention or otherwise, by any usage or abuse of any policies, processes, or directions contained within is the solitary and utter responsibility of the recipient reader. Under no circumstances will any legal responsibility or blame be held against the publisher for any reparation, damages, or monetary loss due to the information herein, either directly or indirectly.

Respective authors own all copyrights not held by the publisher.

The information herein is offered for informational purposes solely, and is universal as so. The presentation of the information is without contract or any type of guarantee assurance.

The trademarks that are used are without any consent, and the publication of the trademark is without permission or backing by the trademark owner. All trademarks and brands within this book are for clarifying purposes only and are the owned by the owners themselves, not affiliated with this document.

Printed in Great Britain
by Amazon